All rights reserved. No part of this publication may be reproduced, distributed, or transmitted in any form or by any means, including photocopying, recording, or other electronic or mechanical methods, without the prior written permission of the publisher, except in the case of brief quotations embodied in critical reviews and certain other non-commercial uses permitted by copyright law.

Prancing Peacock

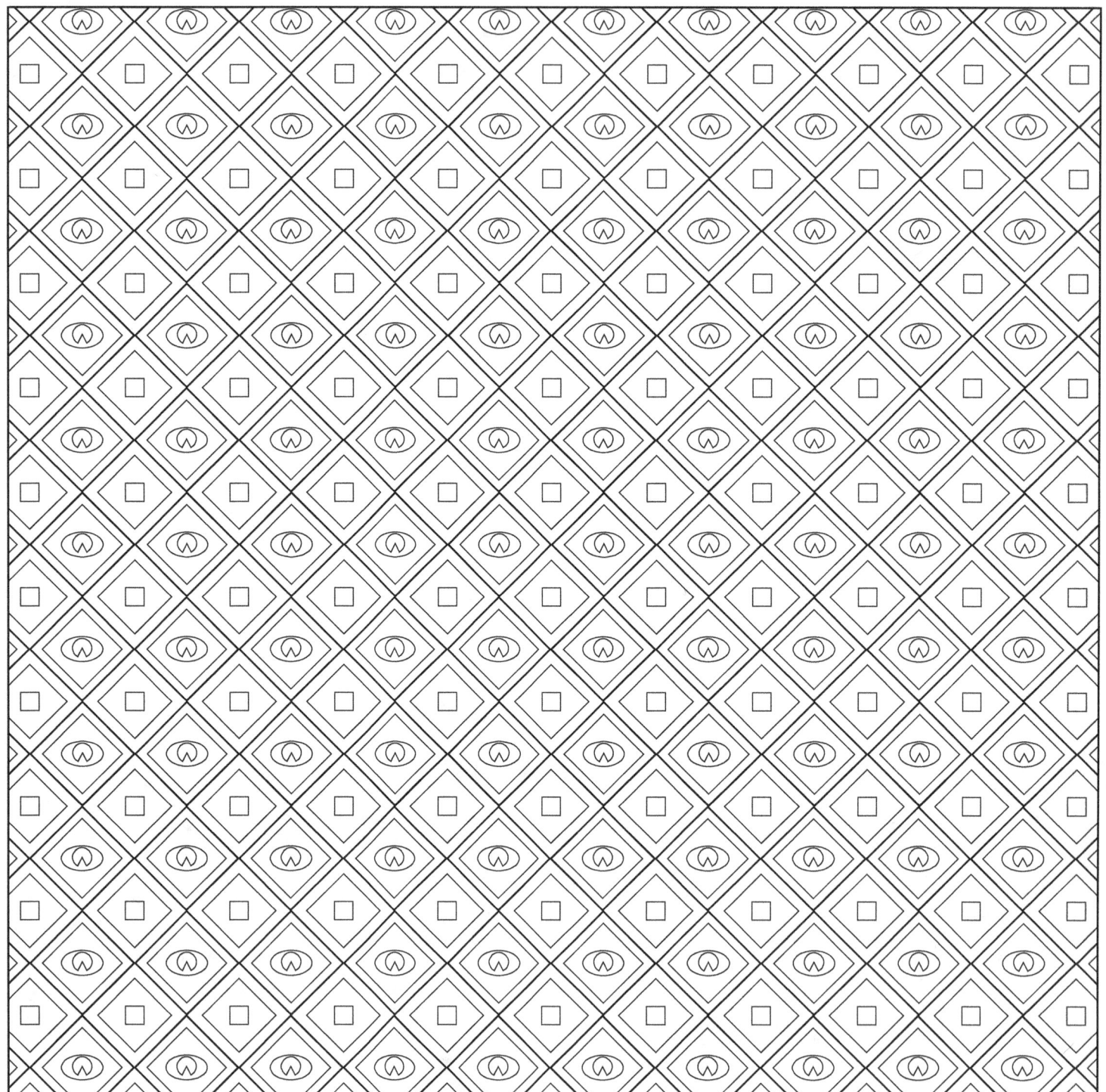

"A peacock that rests on his feathers is just another turkey"
Dolly Parton

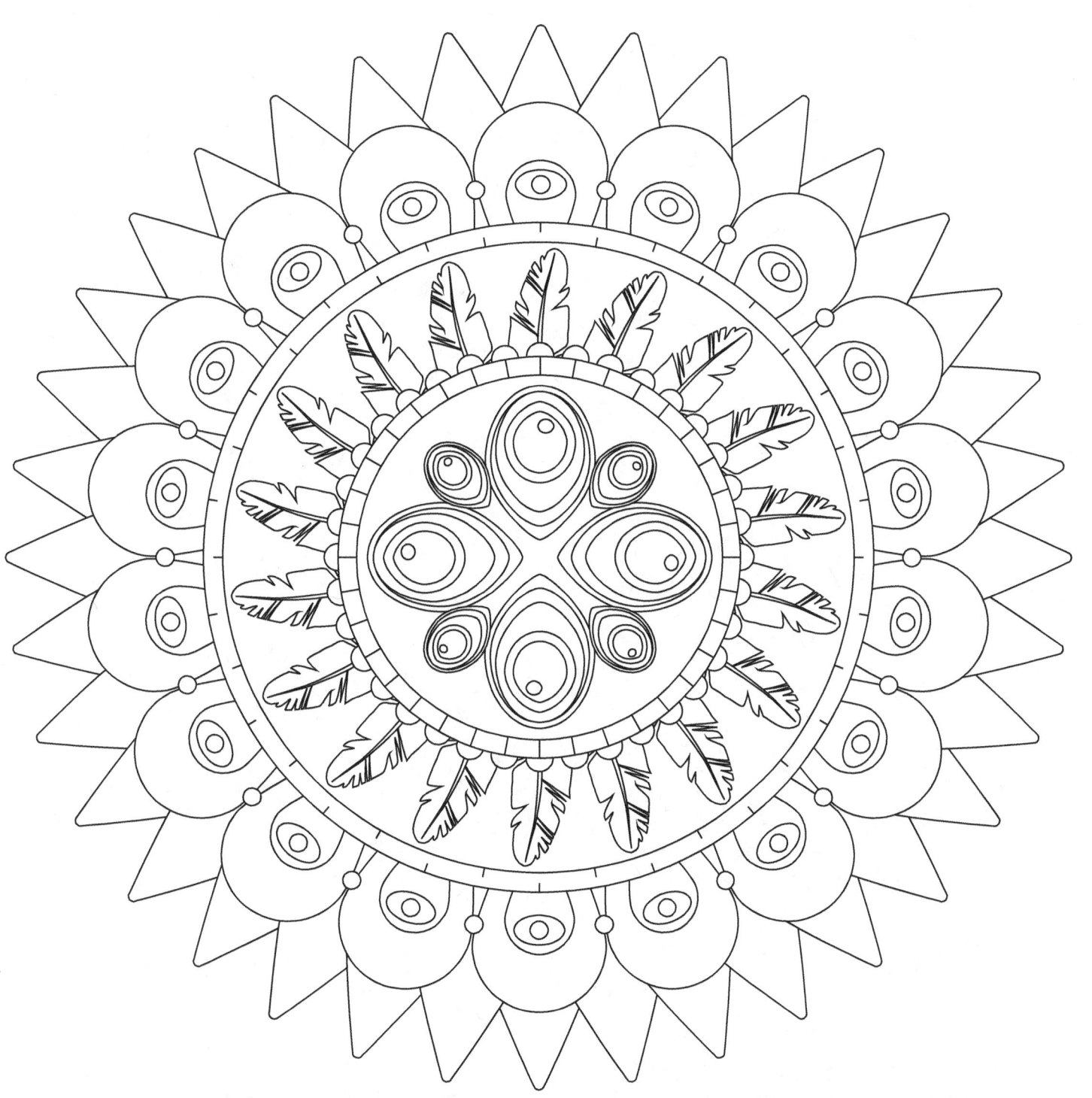

Floral Fantasy

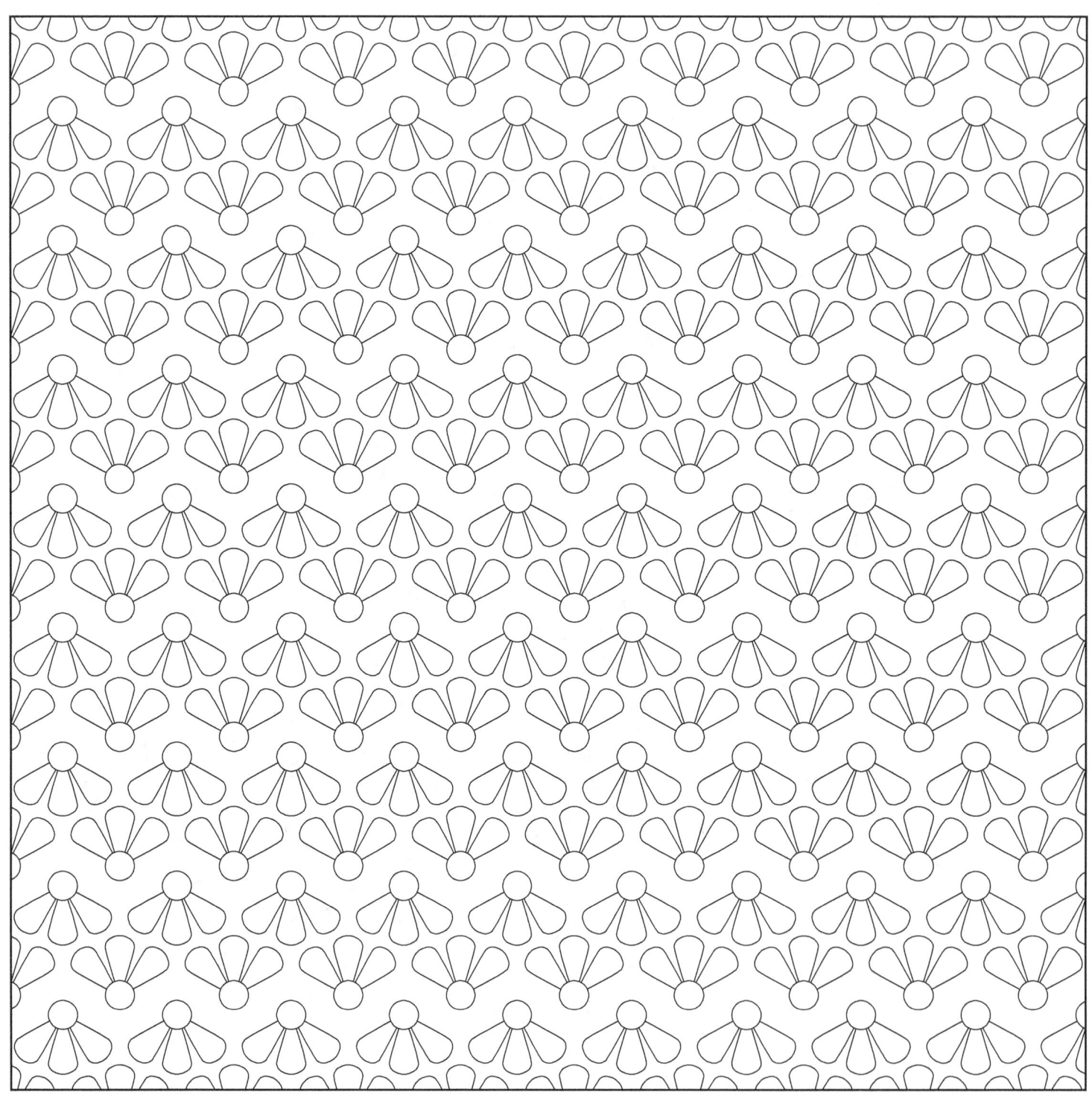

"There are always flowers for those who want to see them"
Henri Matisse

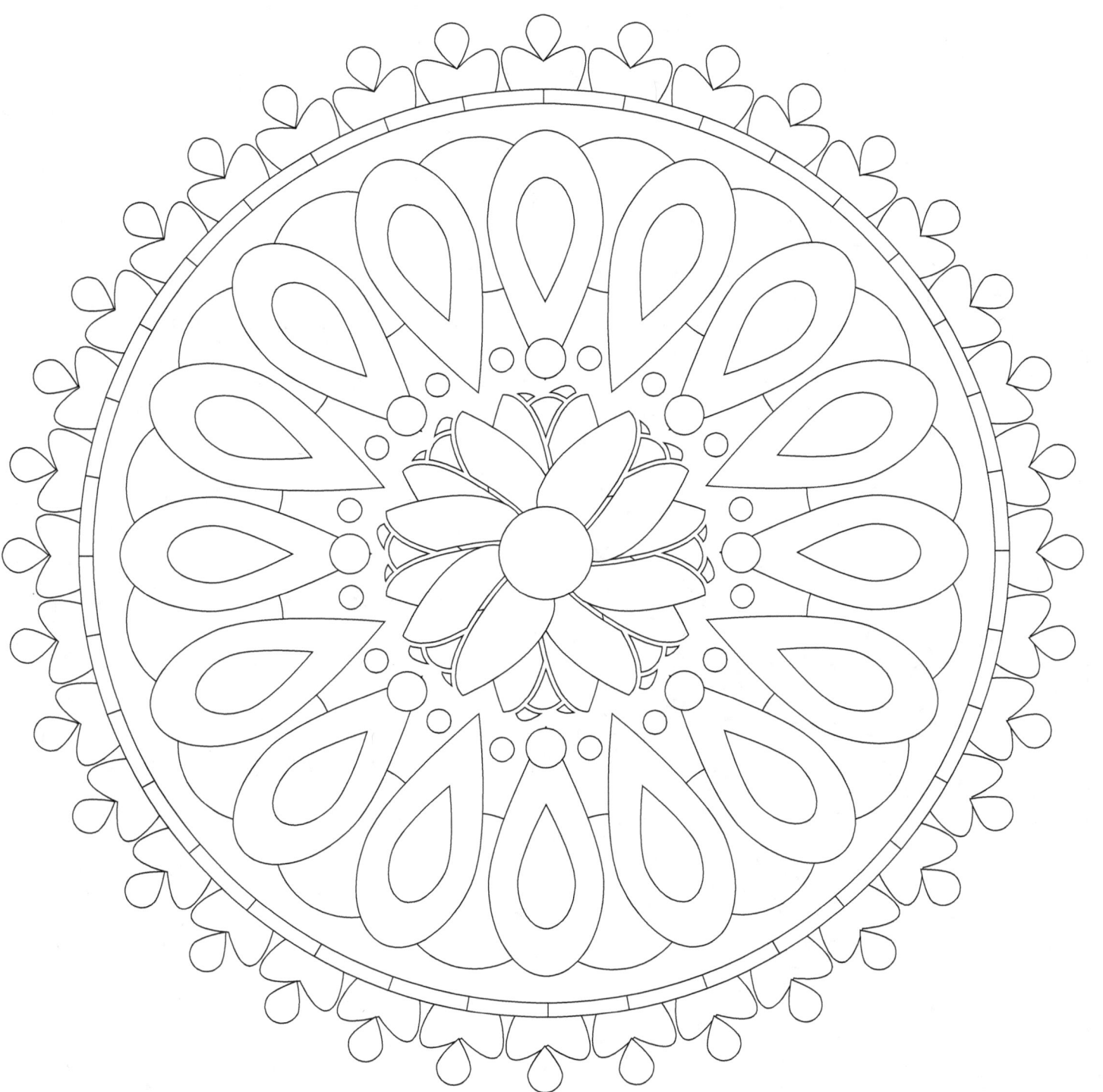

Into the Wild

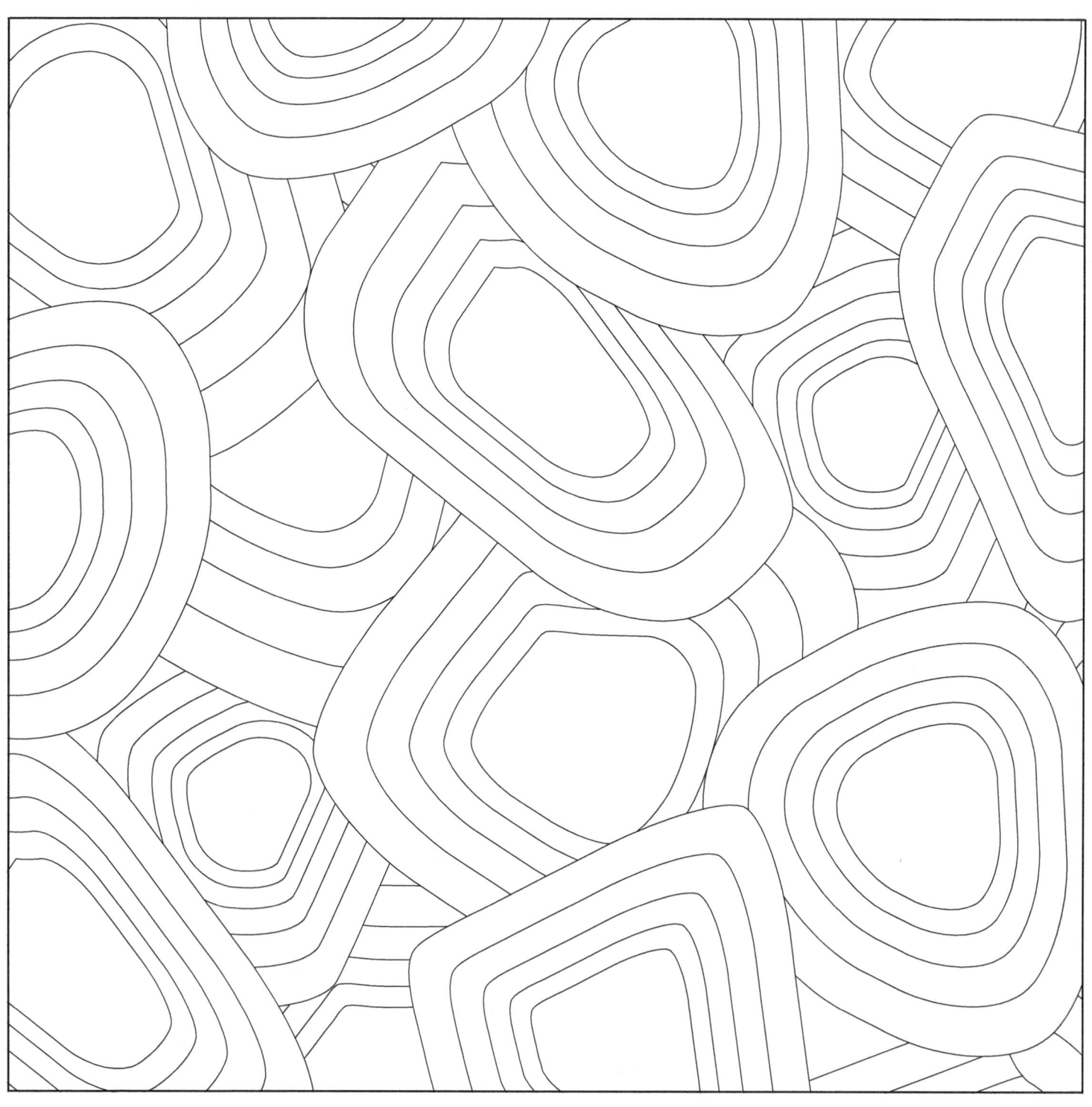

"Animals aren't wild, they are just free"
Native American proverb

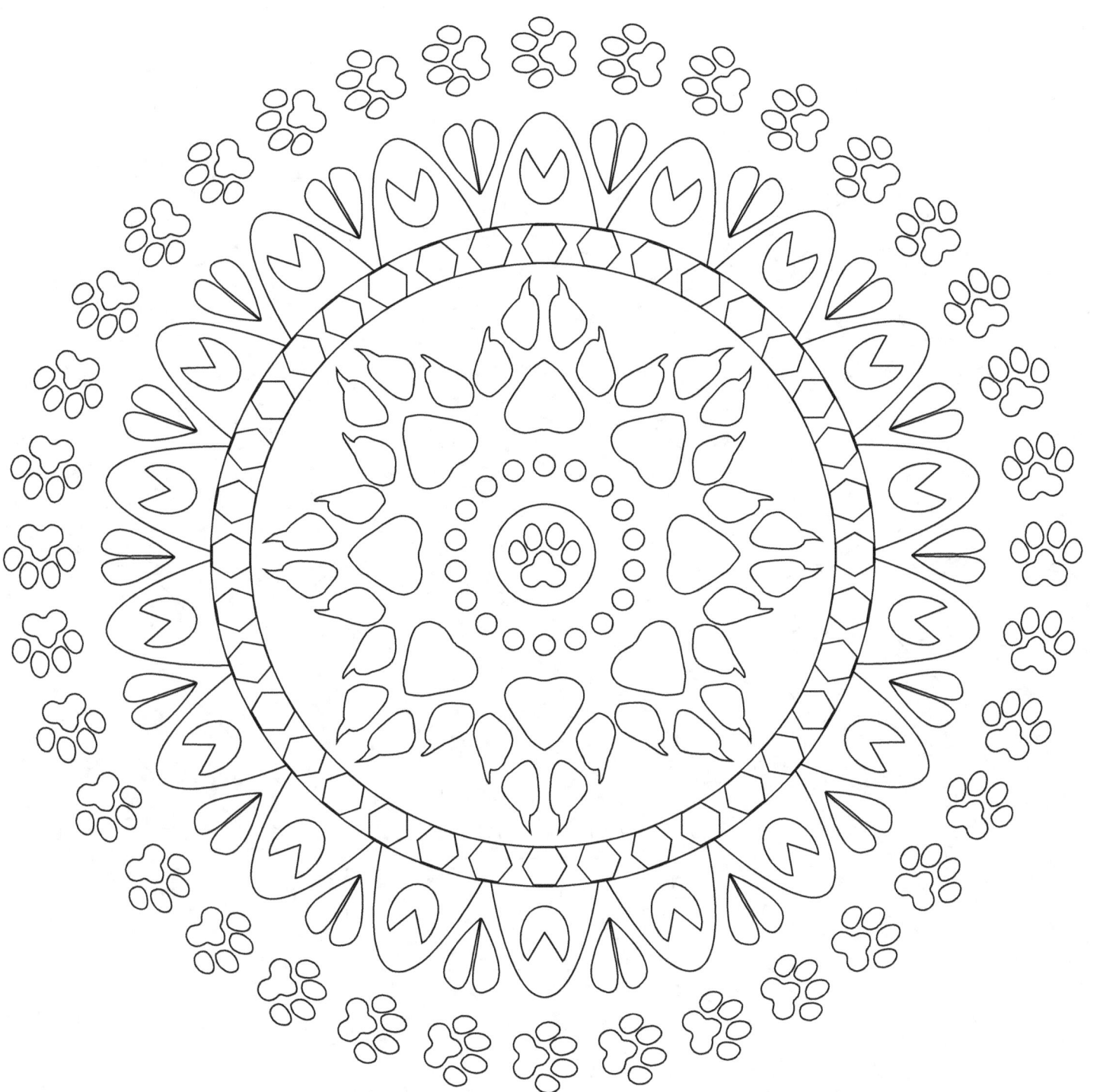

Majestic Mountains

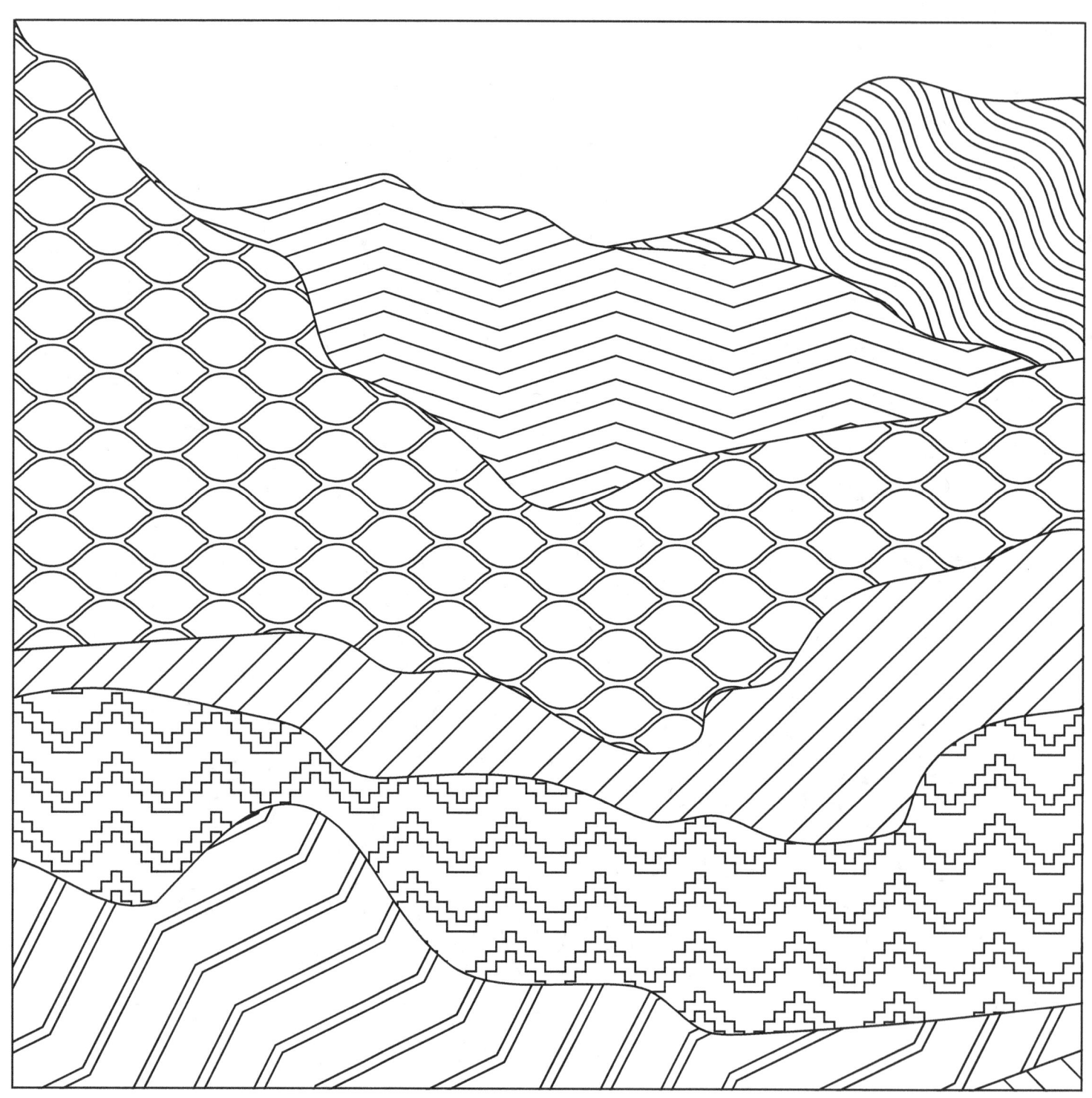

"Climb mountains not so the world can see you,
but so you can see the world."

David McCullough Jr.

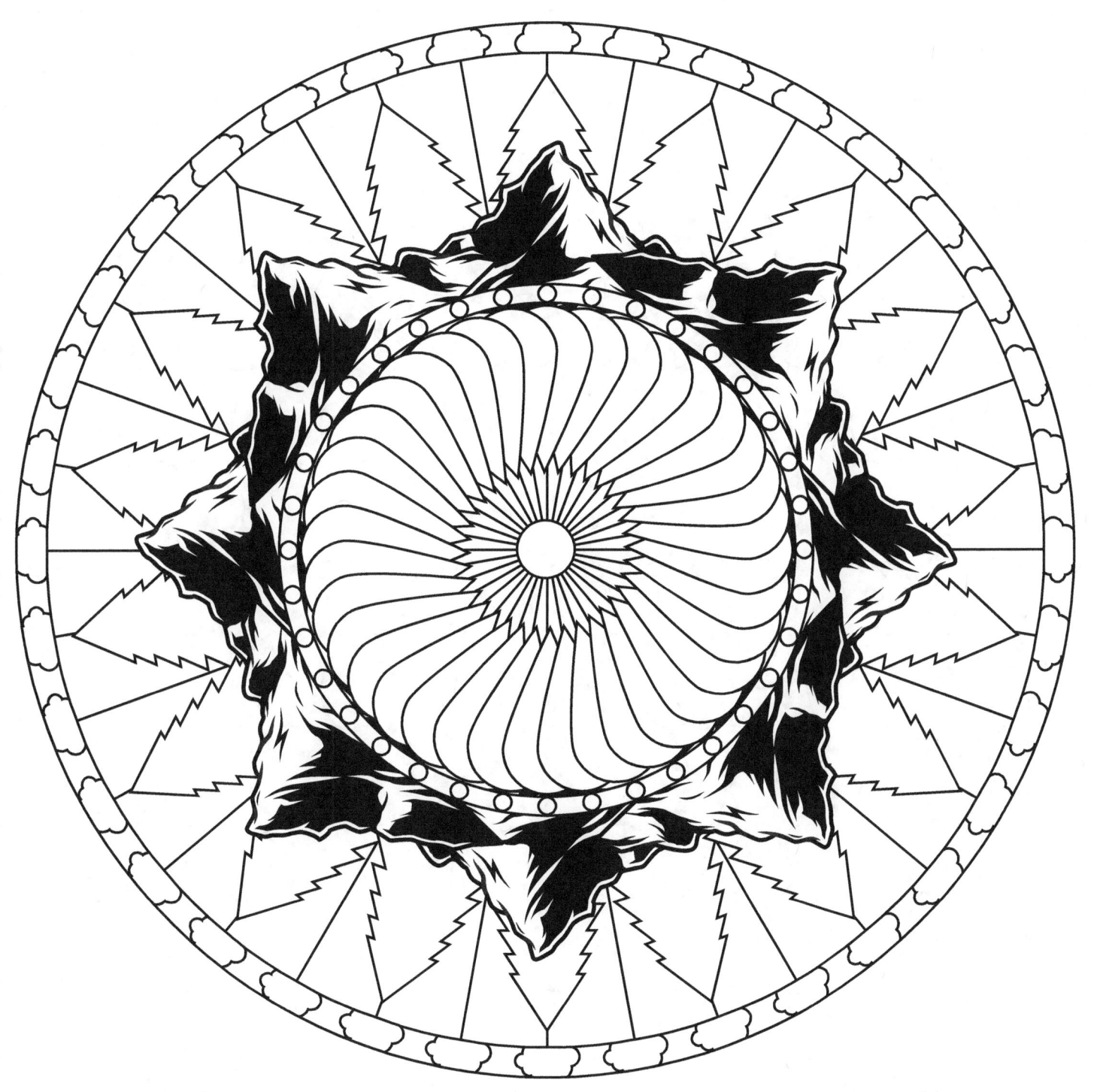

Petal Perfect

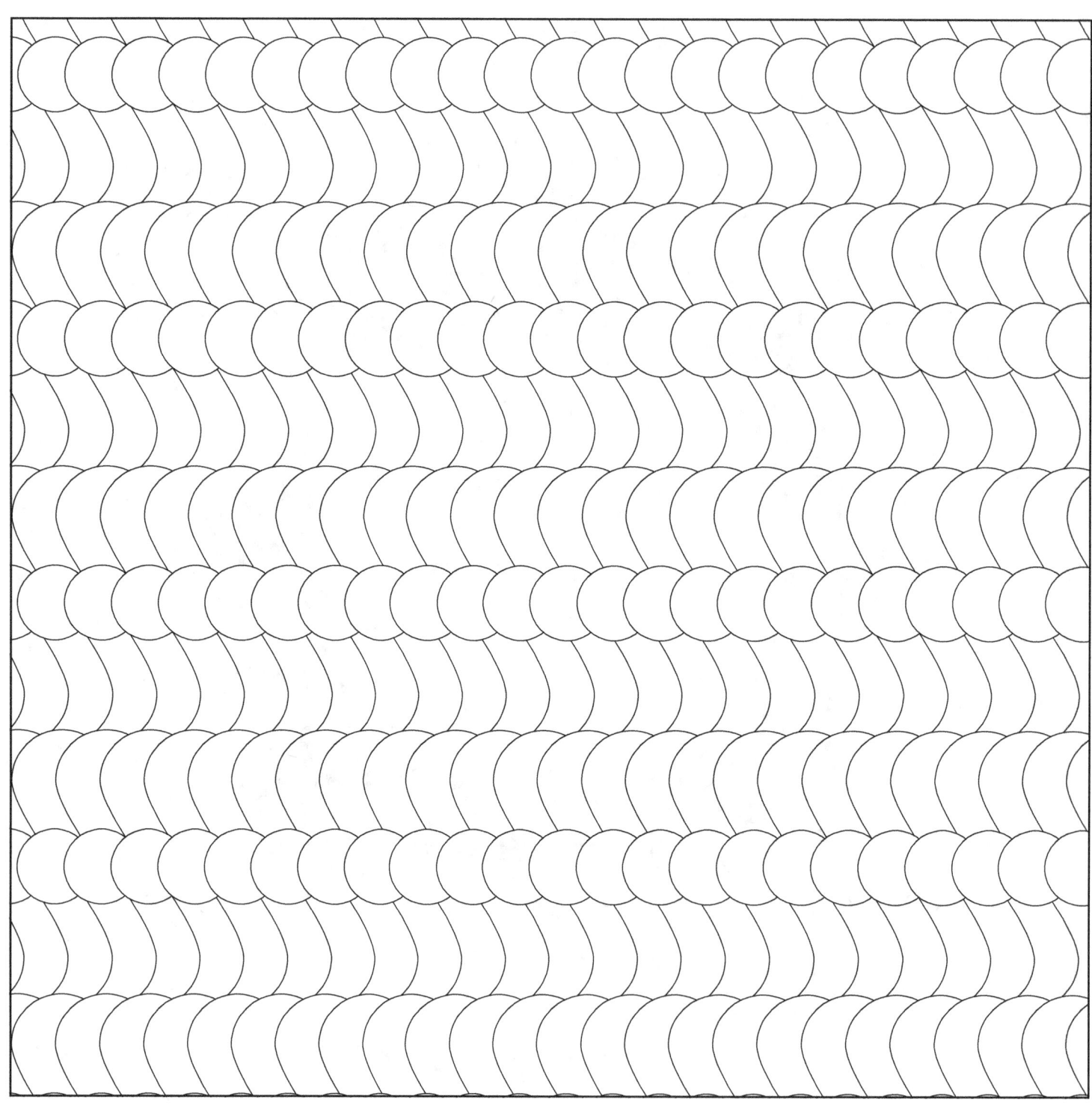

"When the petals of the heart unfold, fragrance spreads across the valley"
Amit Ray

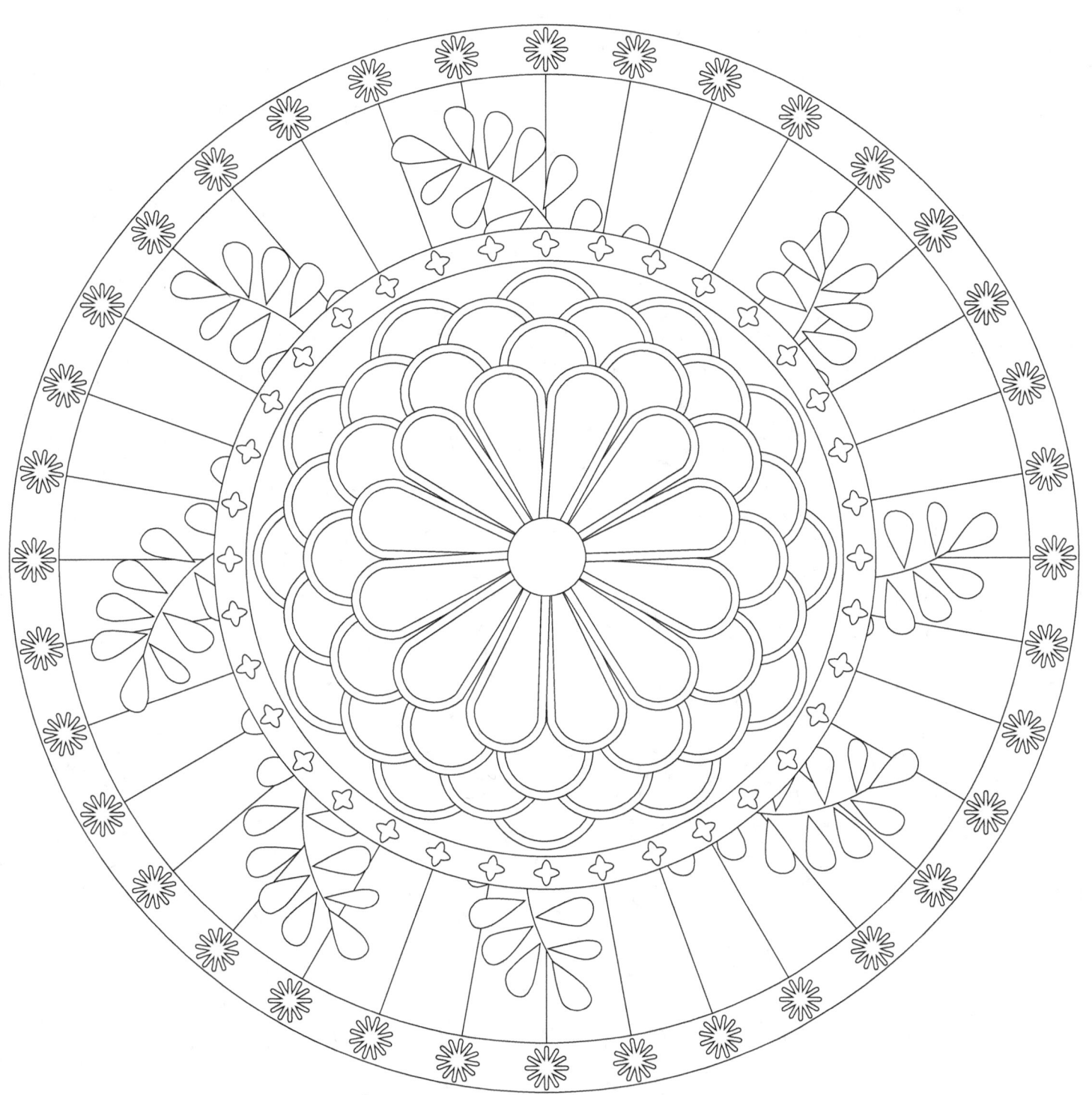

Marvellous Mushrooms

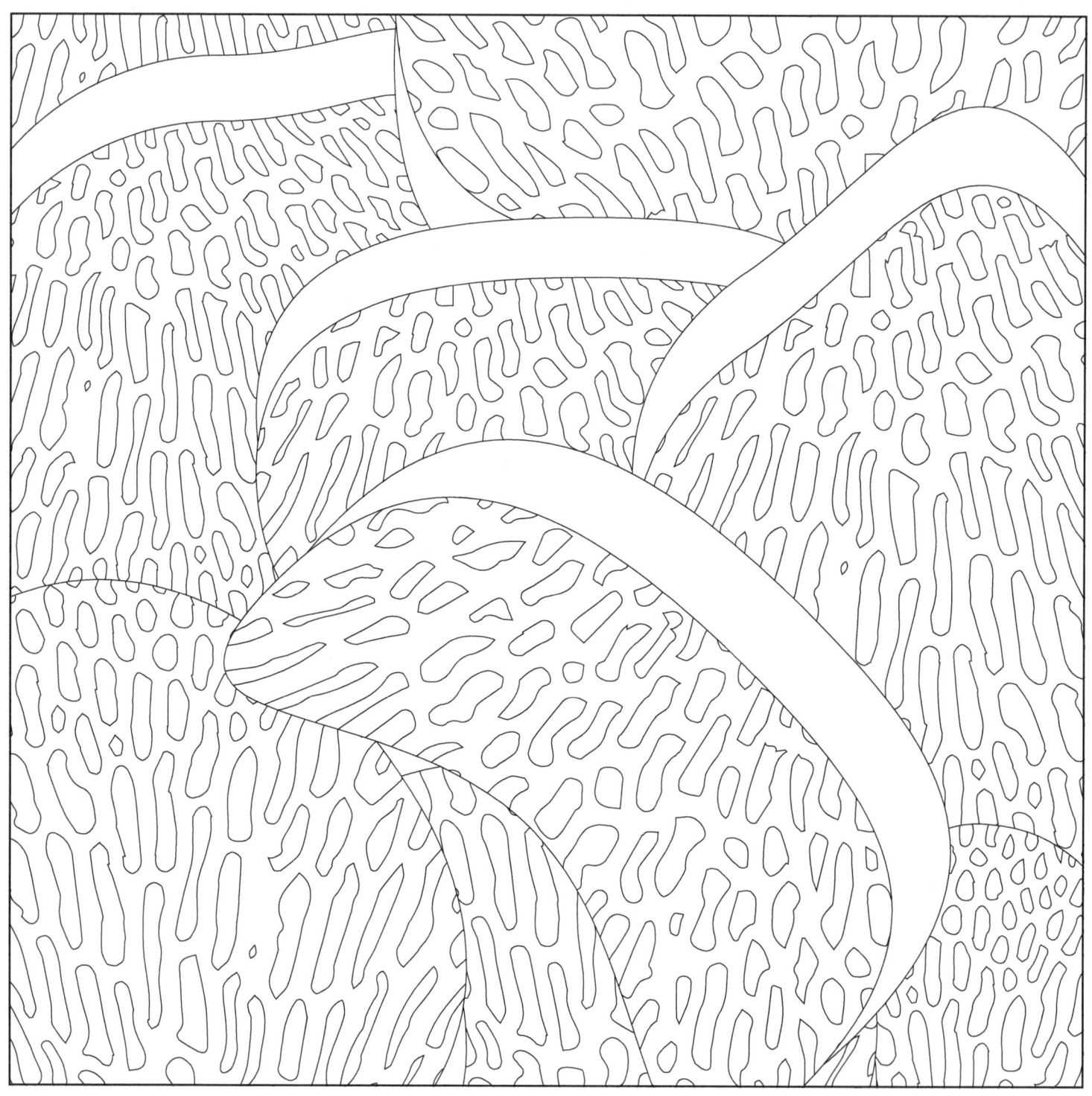

"Nature alone is antique, and the oldest art a mushroom"
Thomas Carlyle

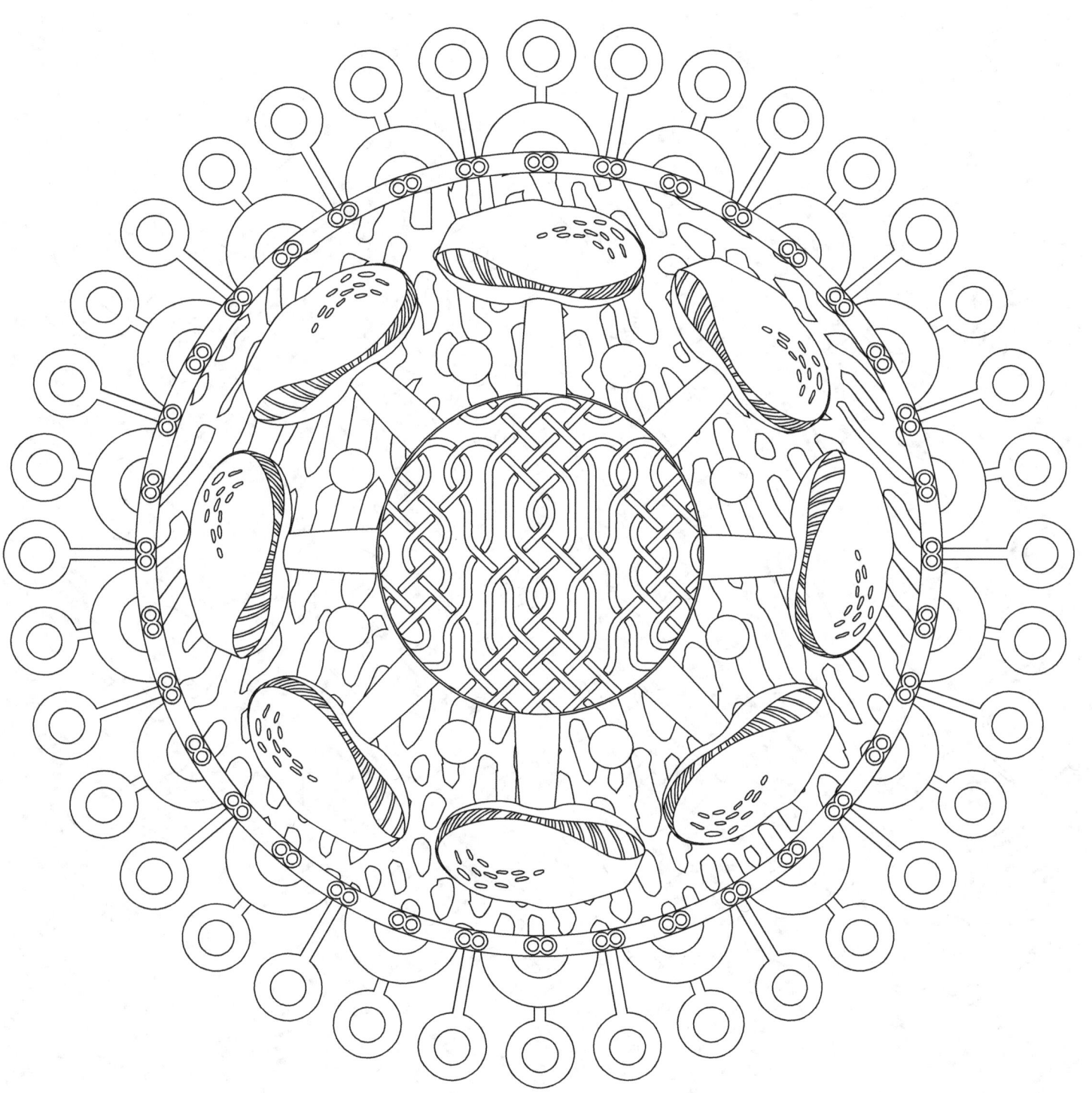

Fine Fish

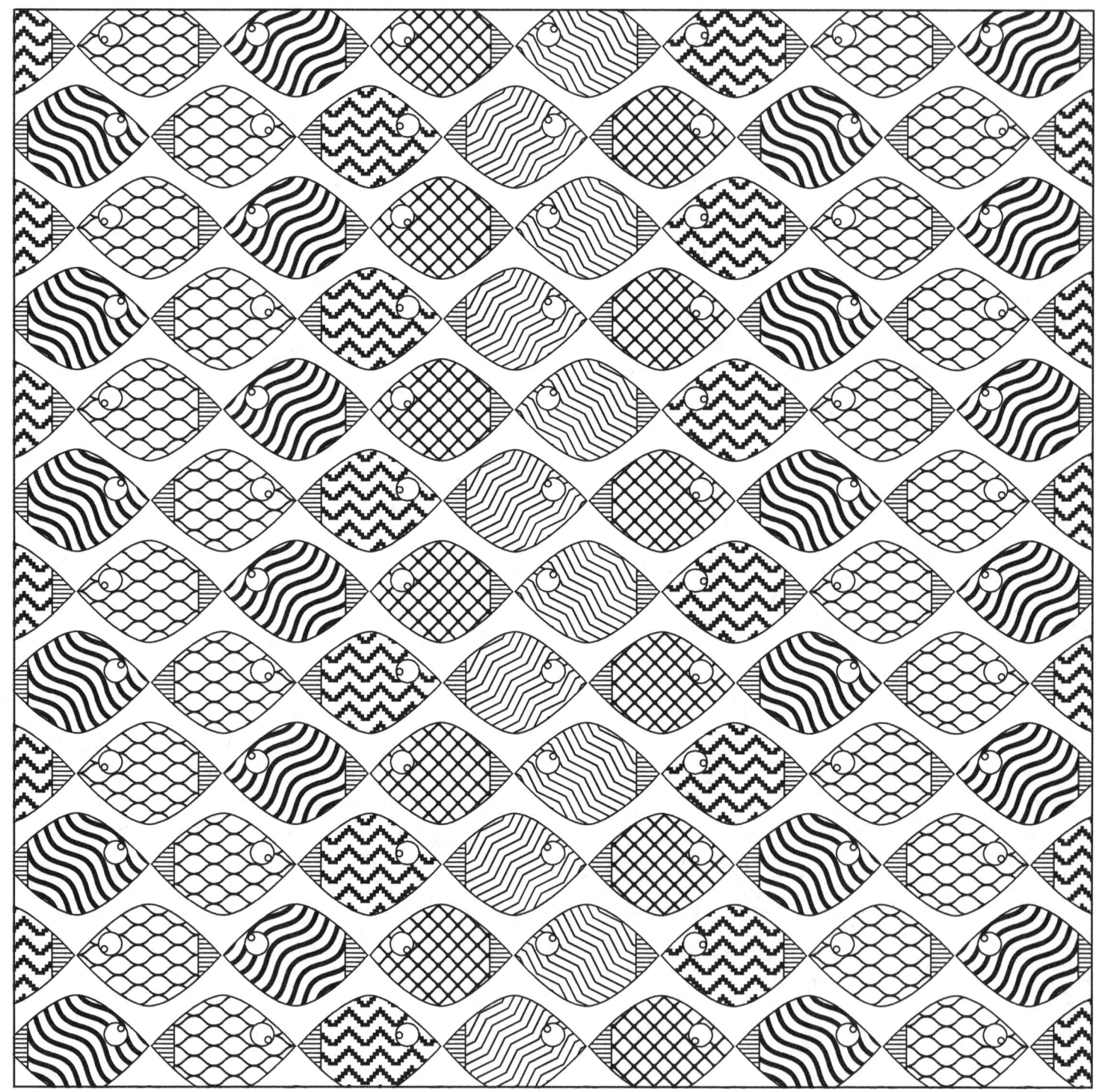

"No wise fish would go anywhere without a porpoise"
Lewis Carroll

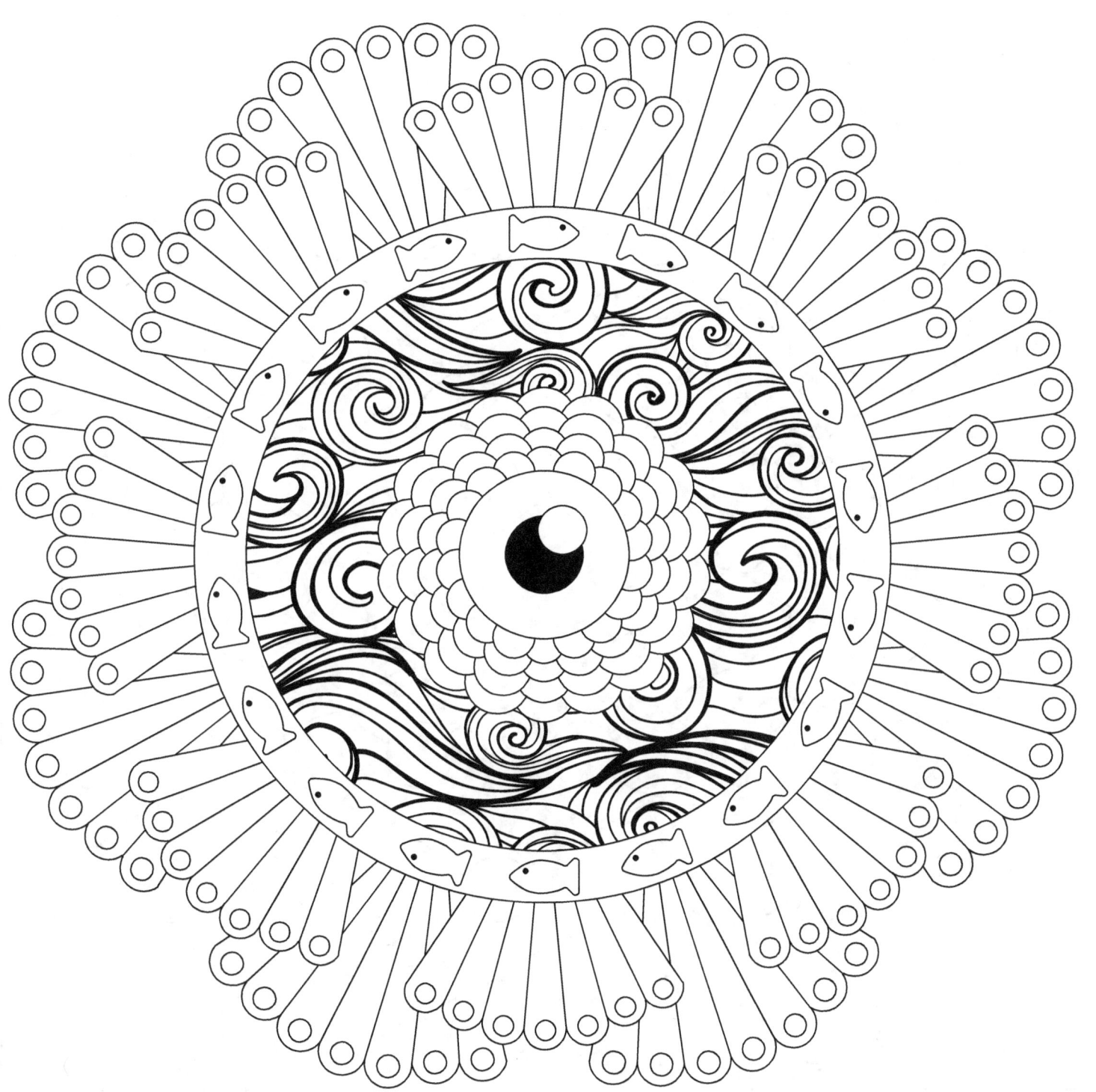

Fair Flower

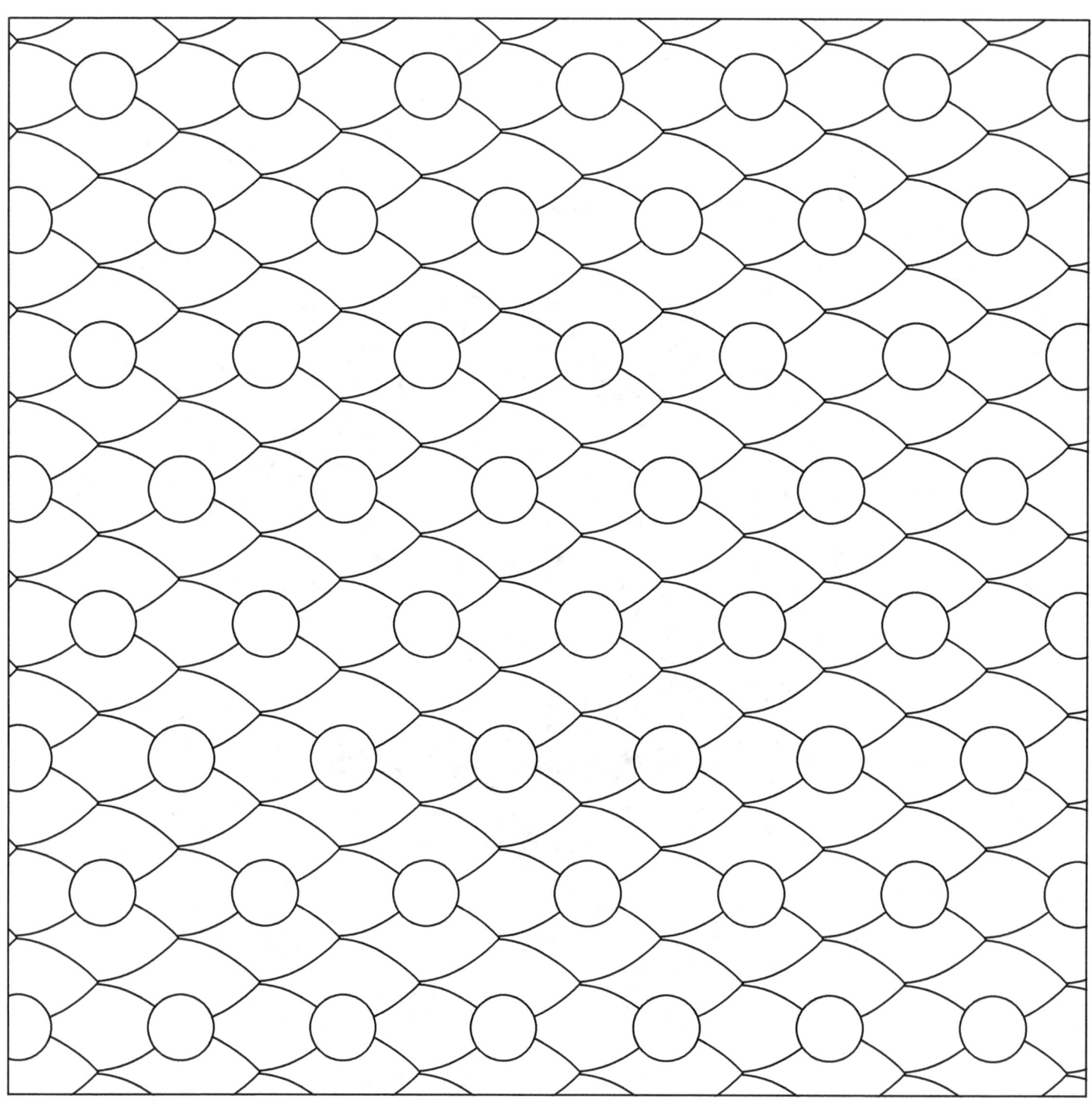

"Even the tiniest of flowers can have the toughest roots"
Shannon Mullen

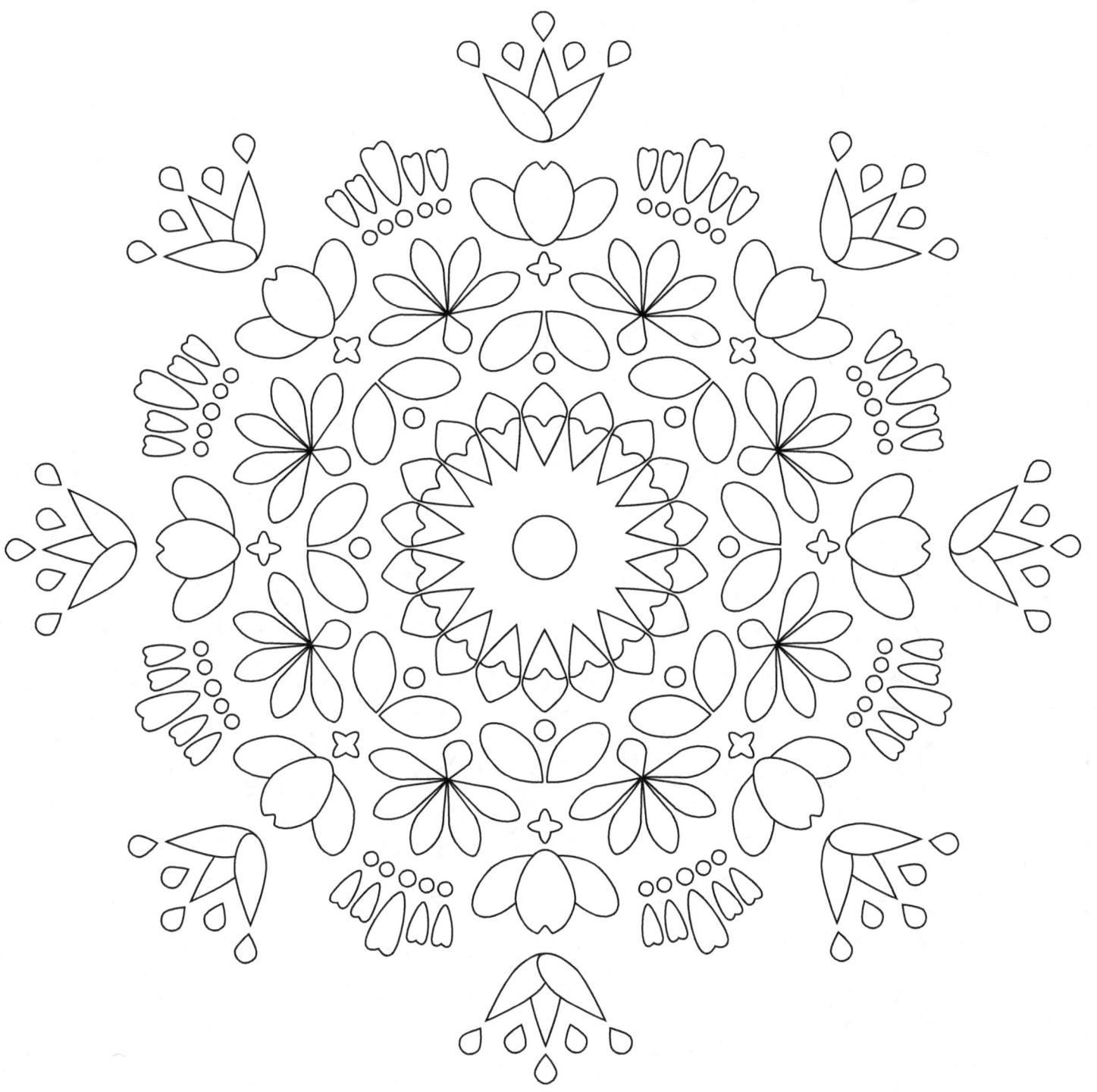

Shoreward Shells

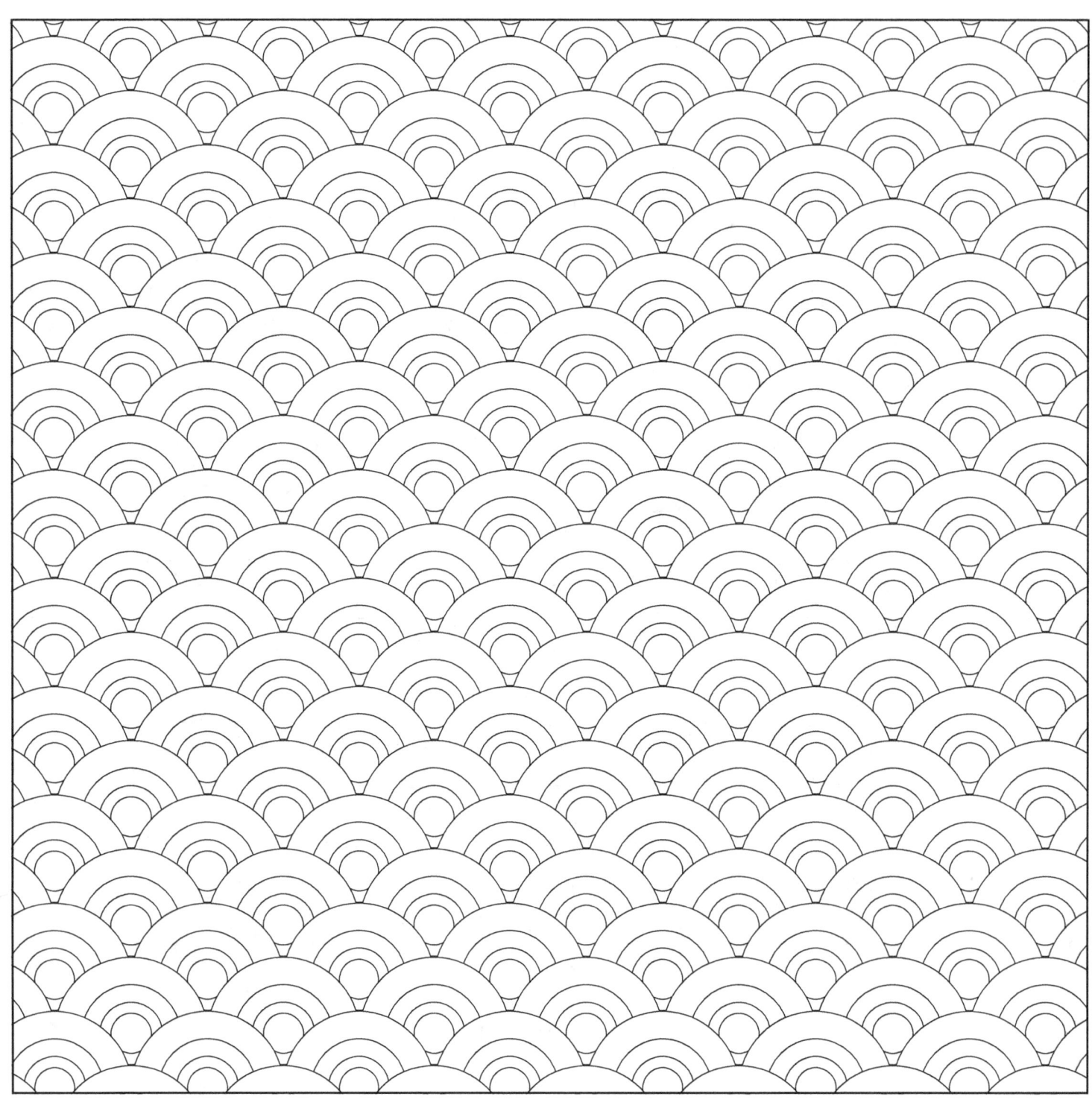

"The flood subsides, and the body, like a worn sea-shell emerges strange and lovely"

D. H. Lawrence

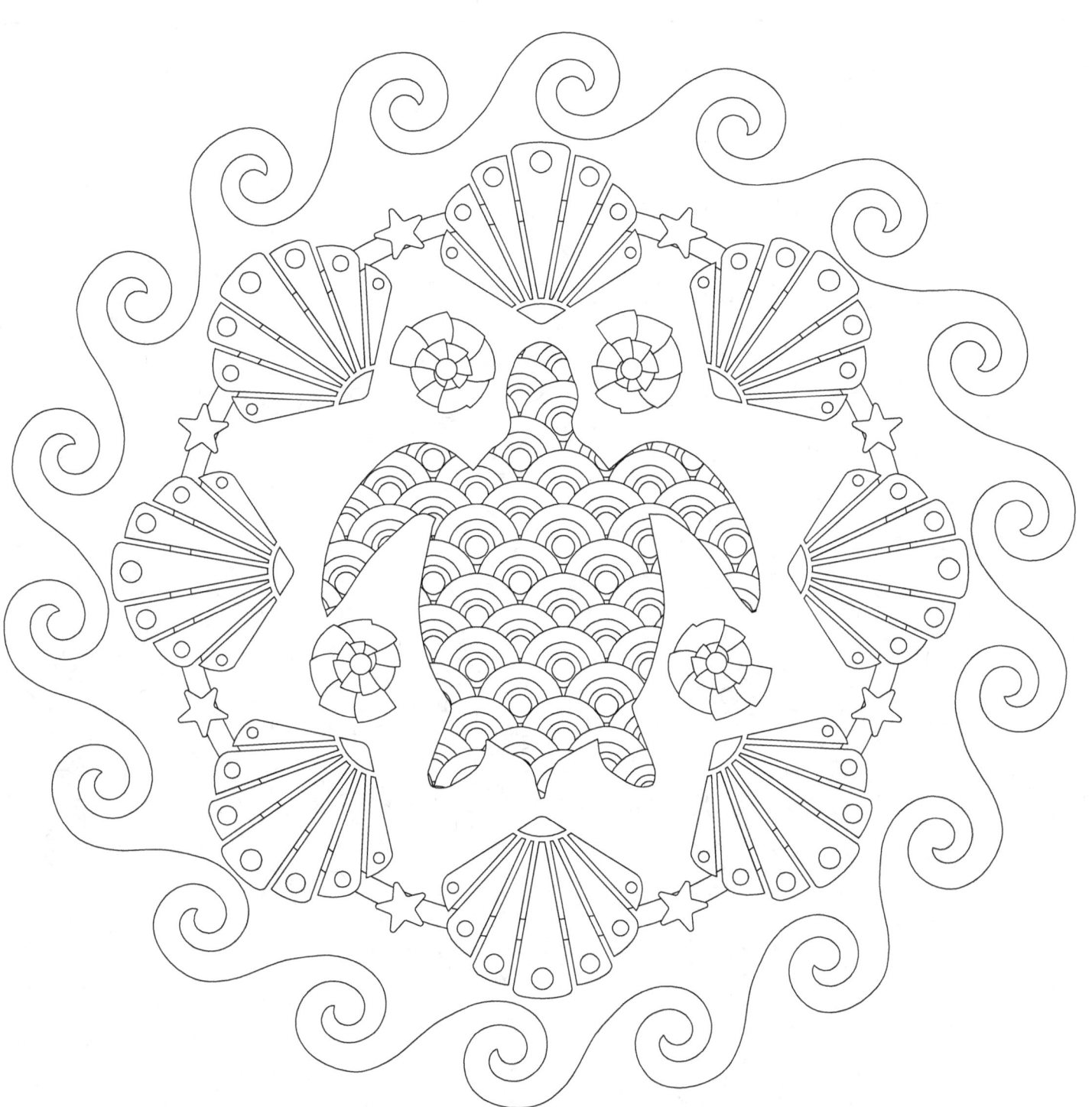

Roaring Jungle

"If man doesn't learn to treat the oceans and the rainforest with respect, man will become extinct."

Peter Benchley

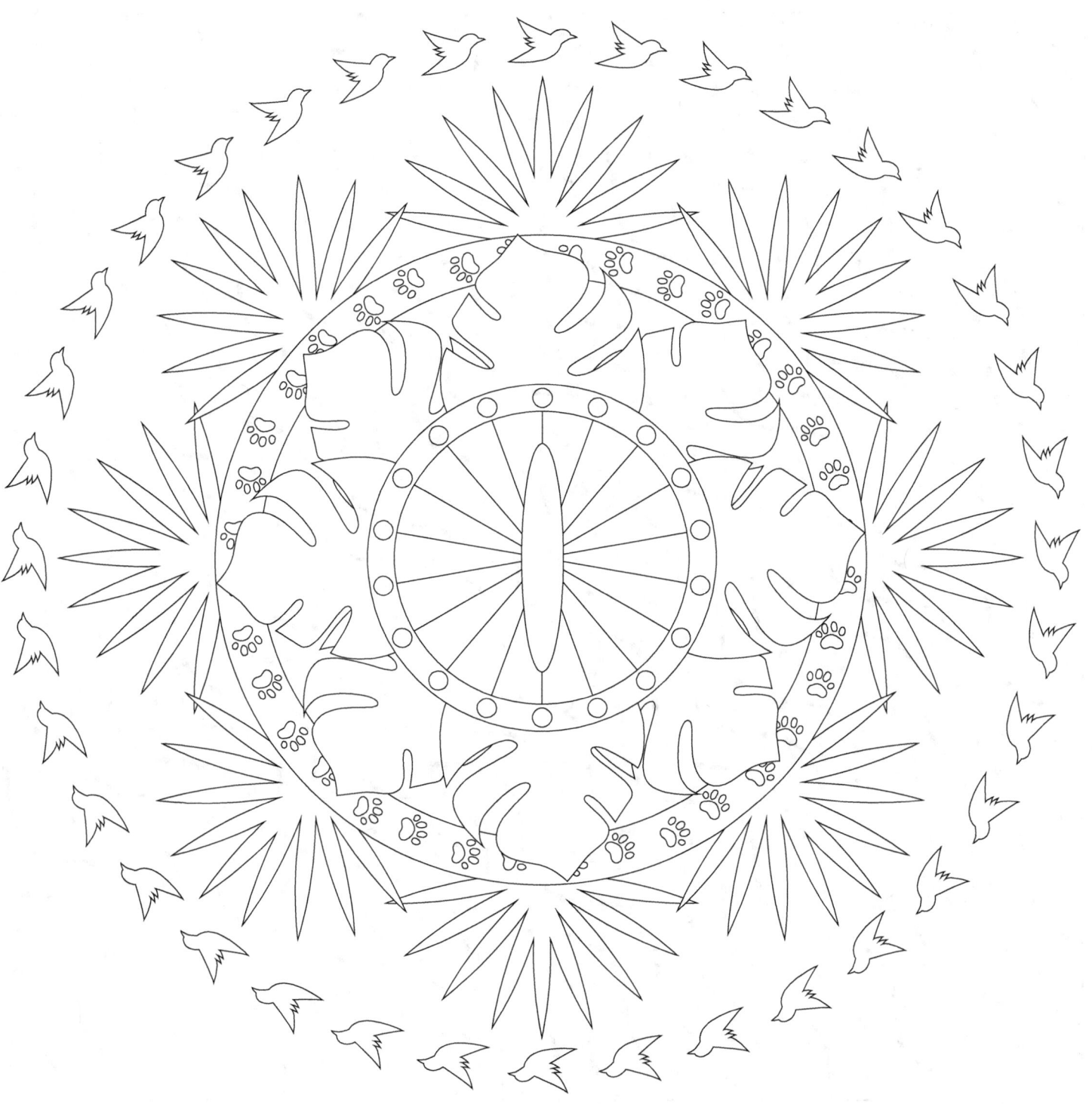

Awesome Ocean

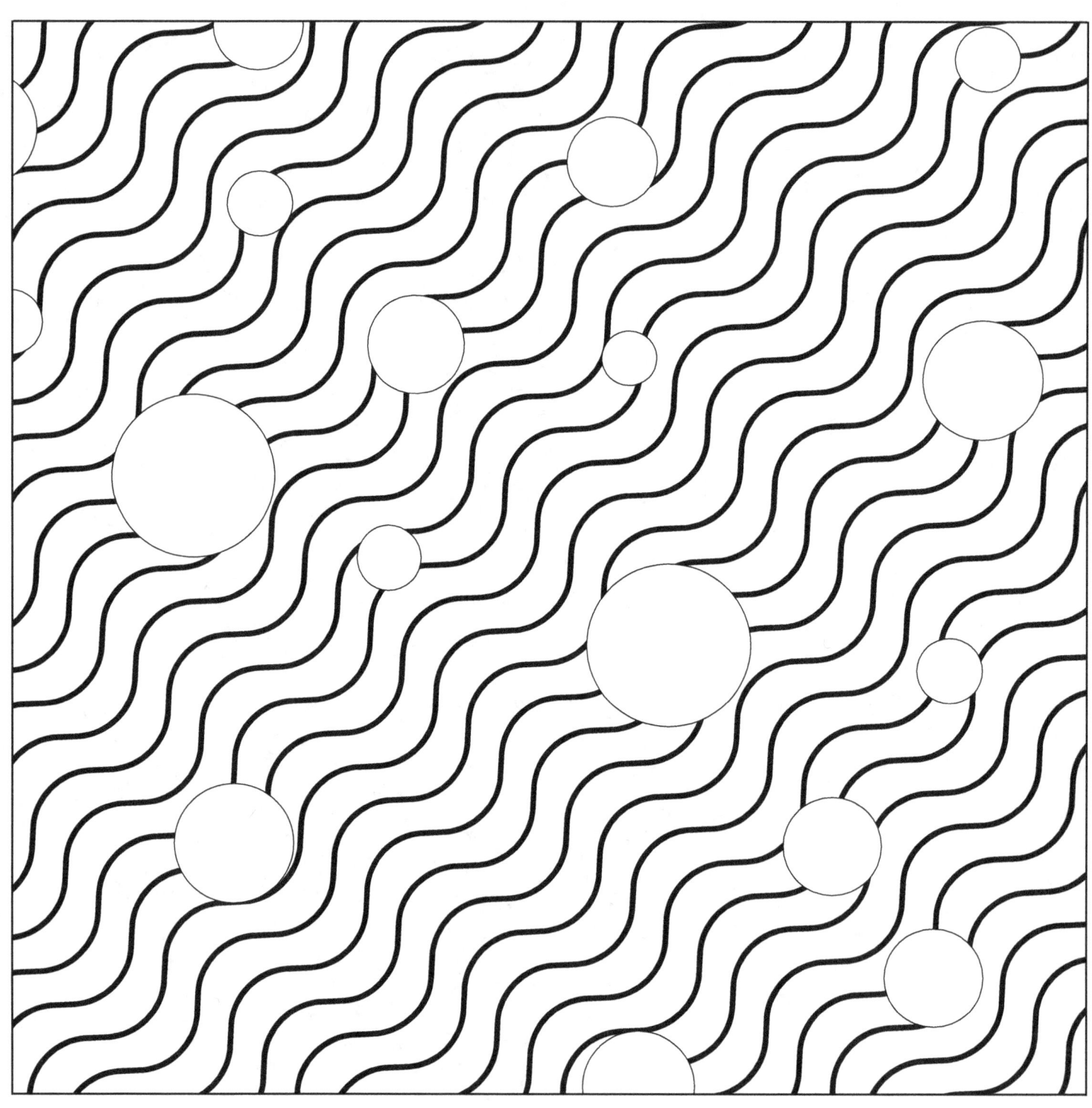

"Humanity is like an ocean; if a few drops of the ocean are dirty, the ocean does not become dirty."

Mahatma Gandhi

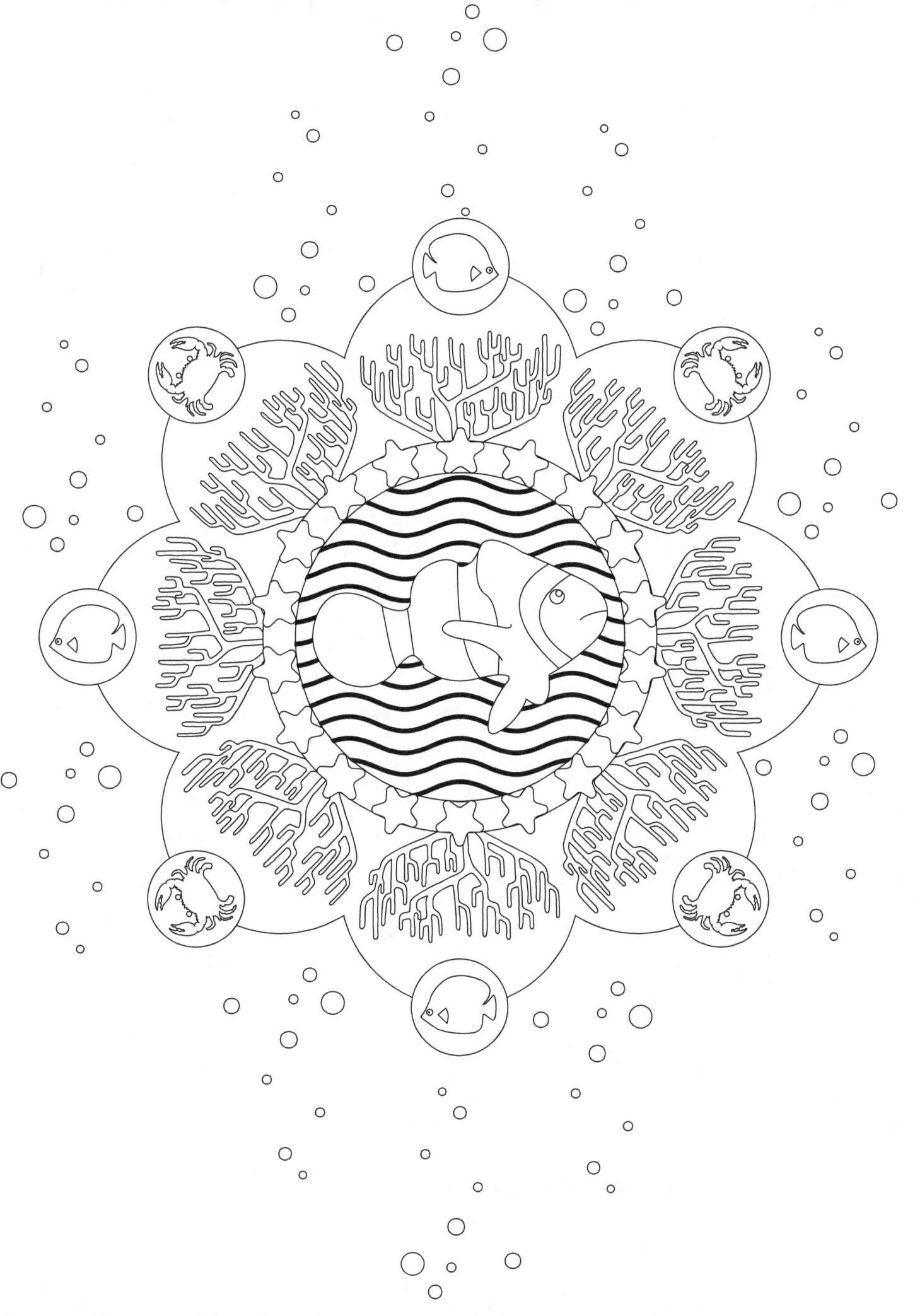

Humble Hare

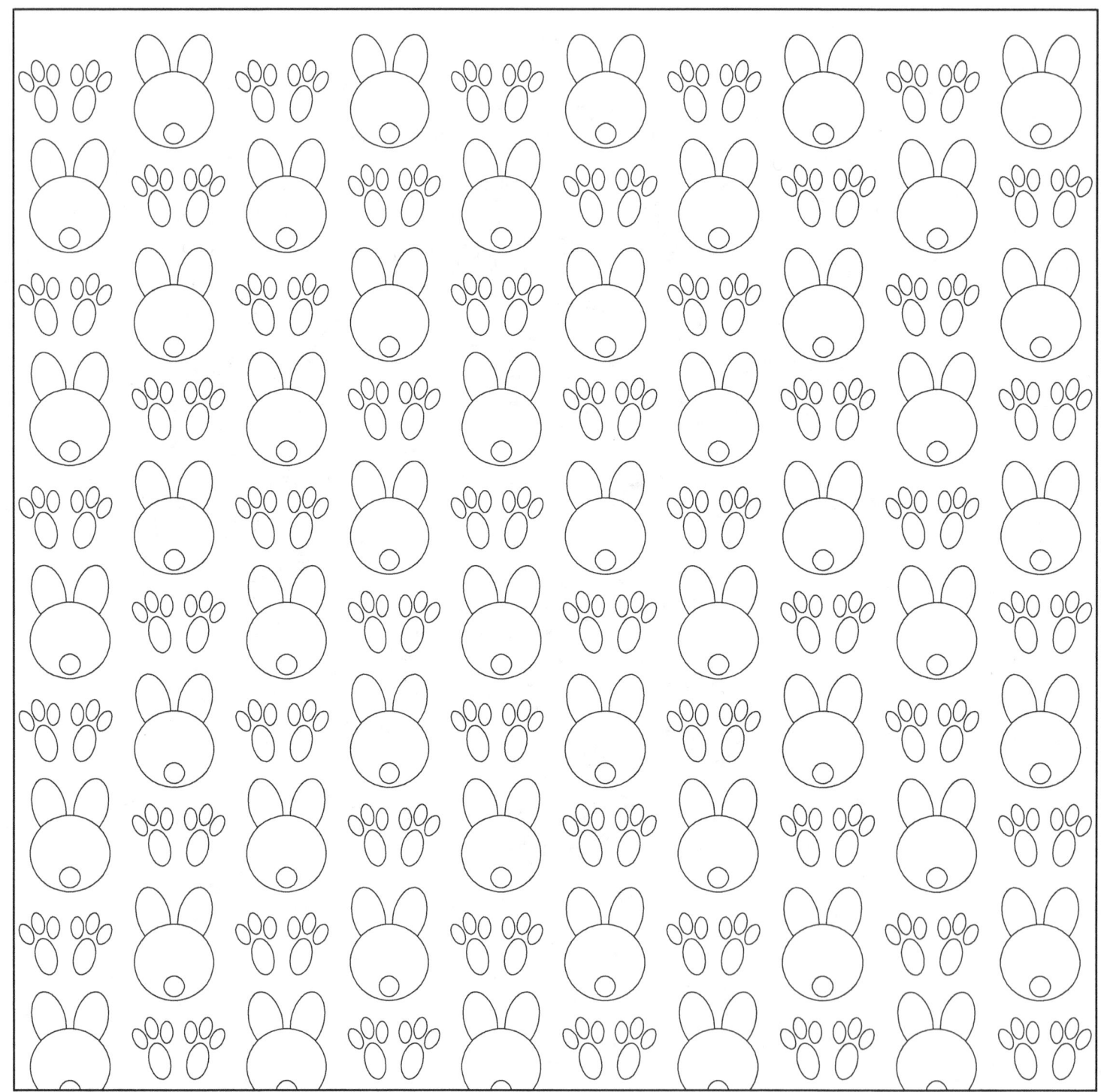

"To cook your hare you must first catch it"

Jean de La Fontaine

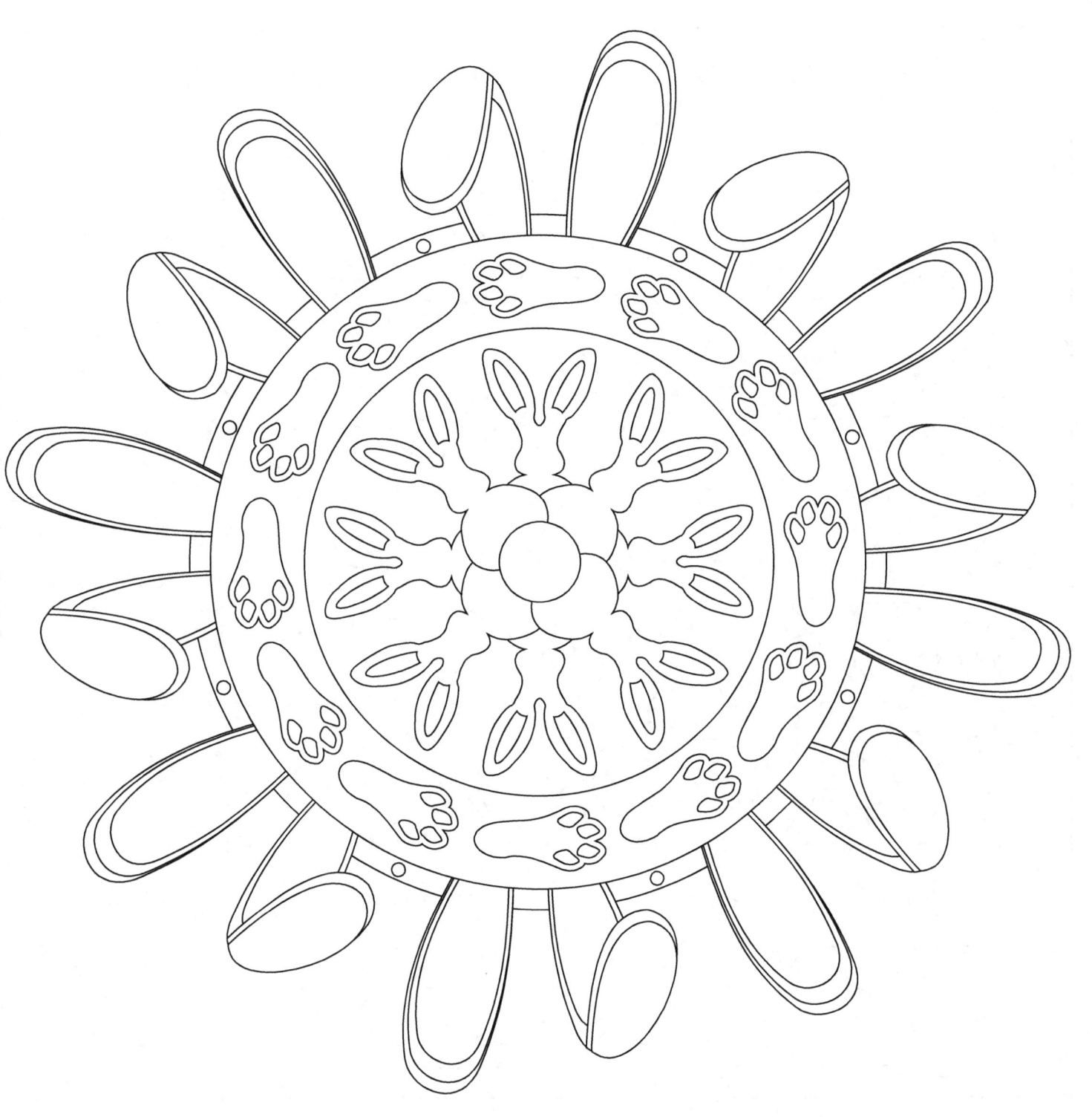

Diamond Dreams

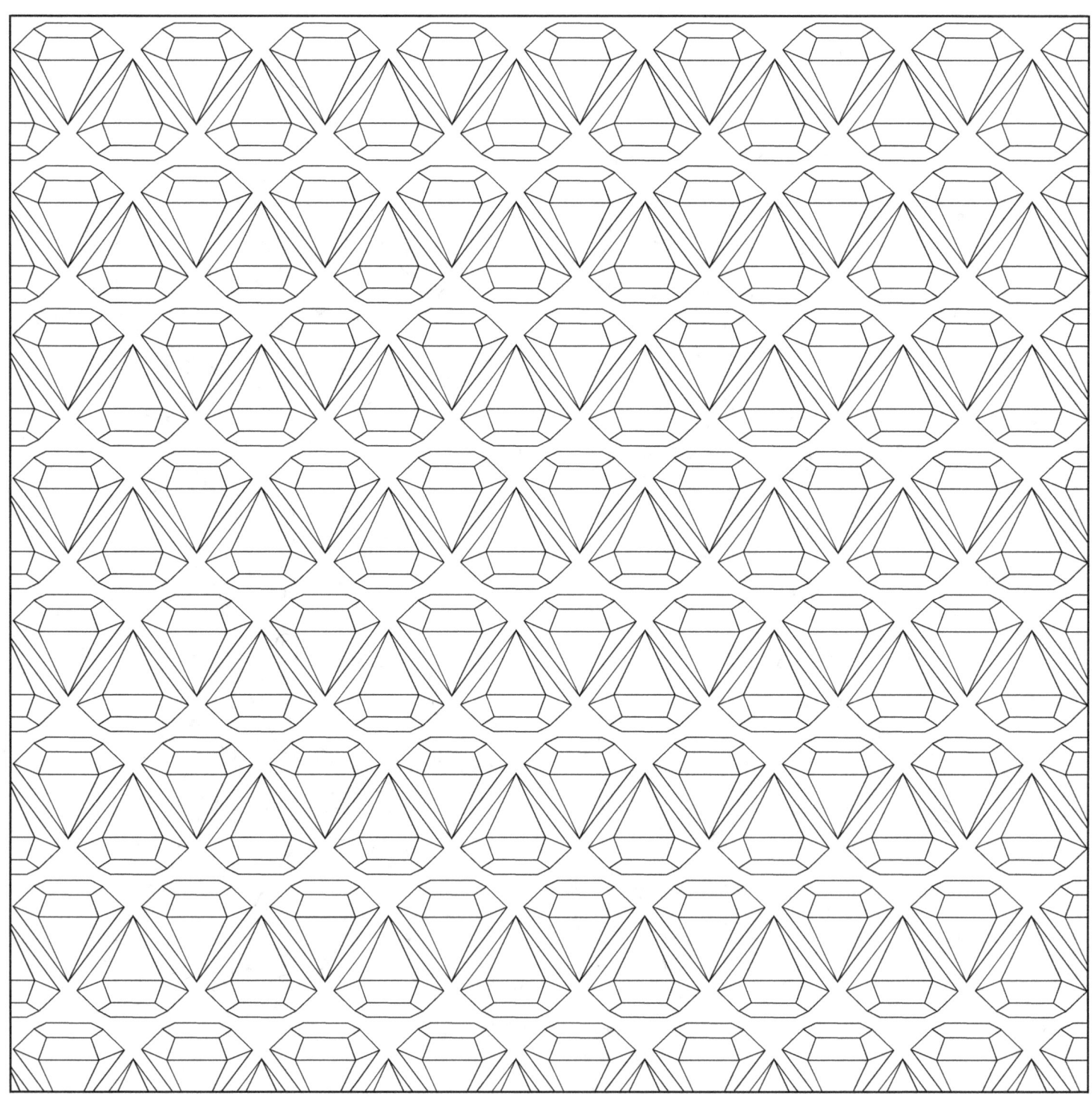

"Remember diamonds are created under pressure so hold on, it will be your time to shine soon"

Sope Agbelusi

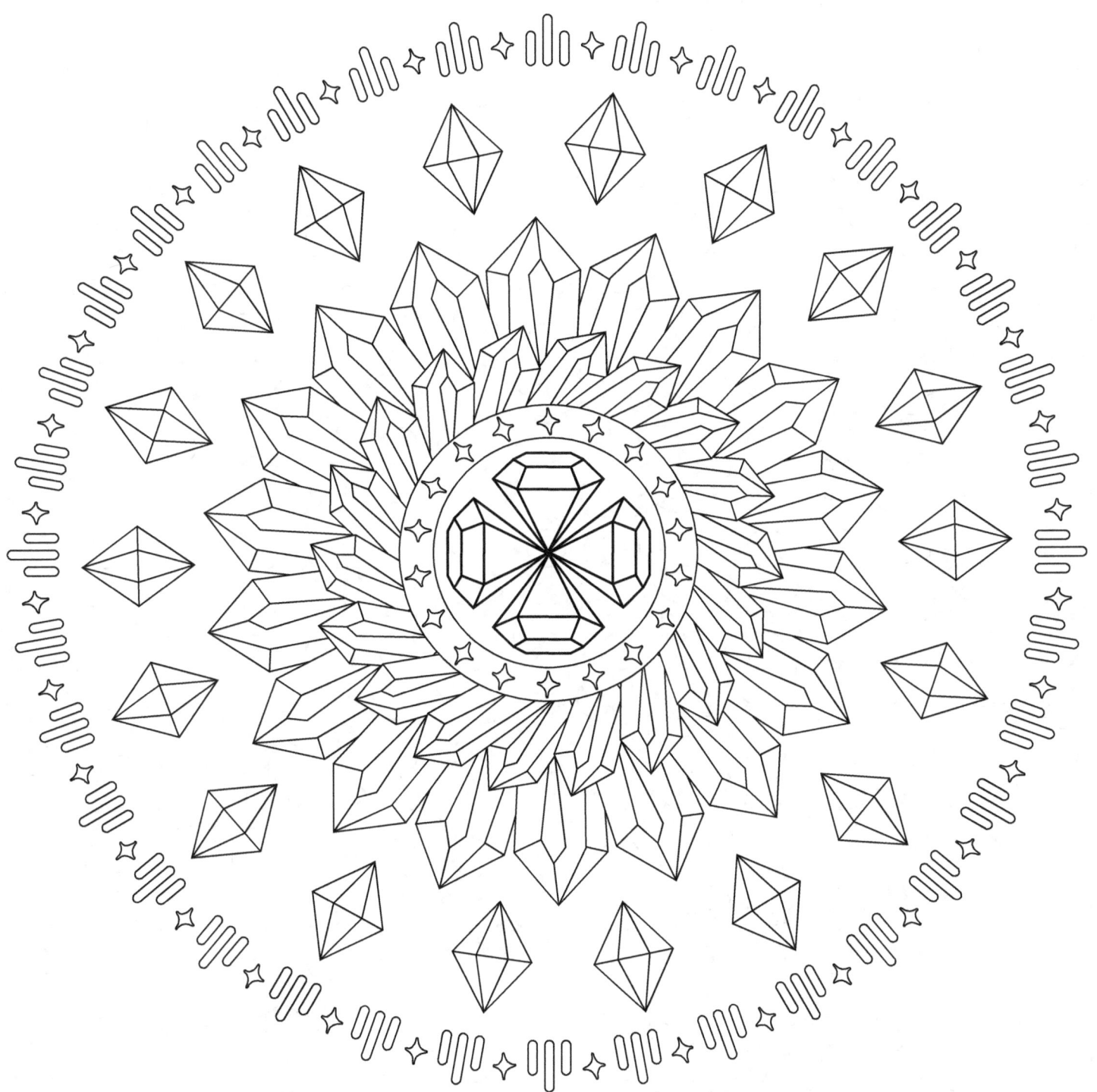

Balmy Beach

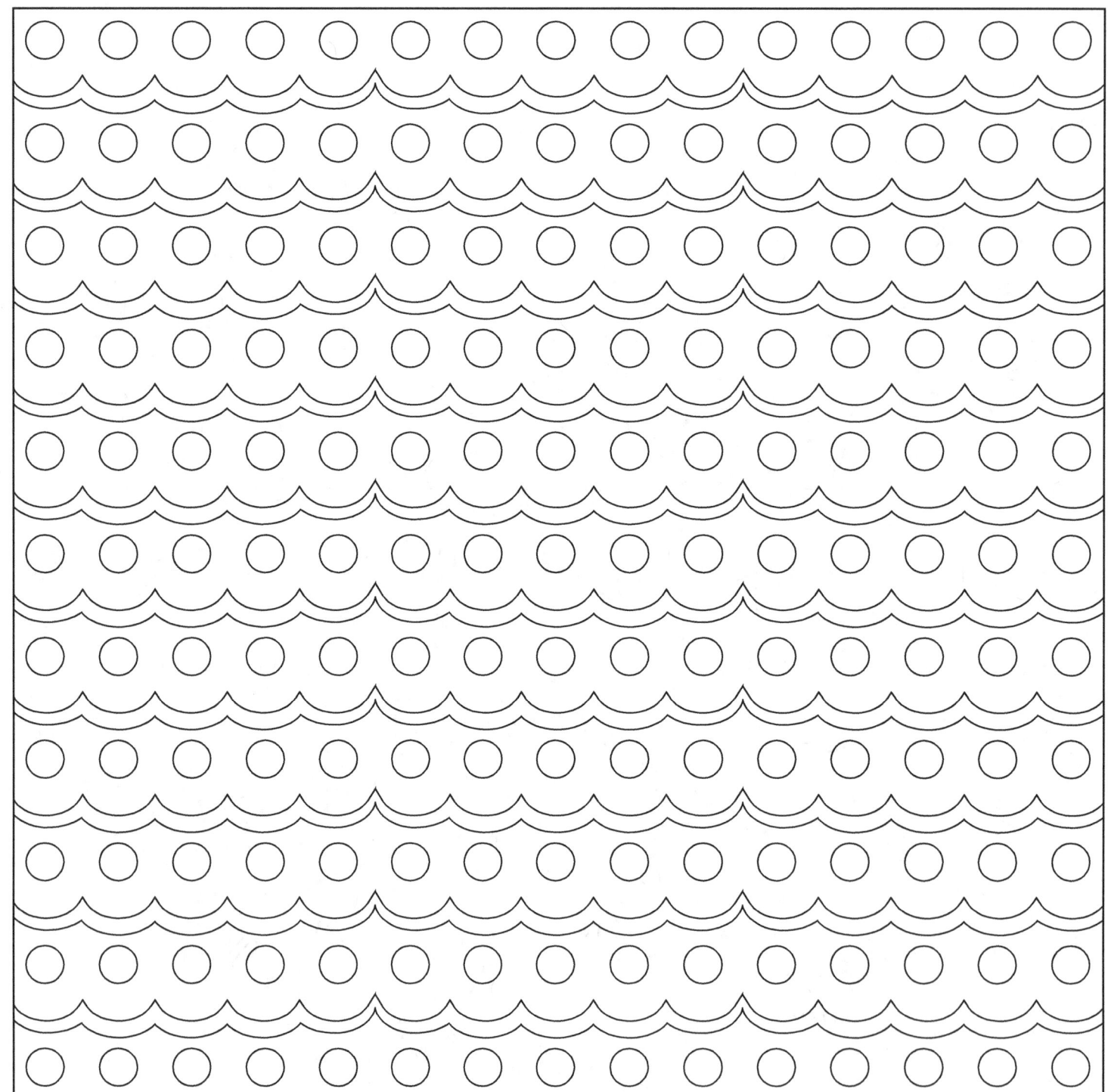

"Our memories of the ocean will linger on, long after our footprints in the sand are gone"

Anonymous

Beautiful Bees

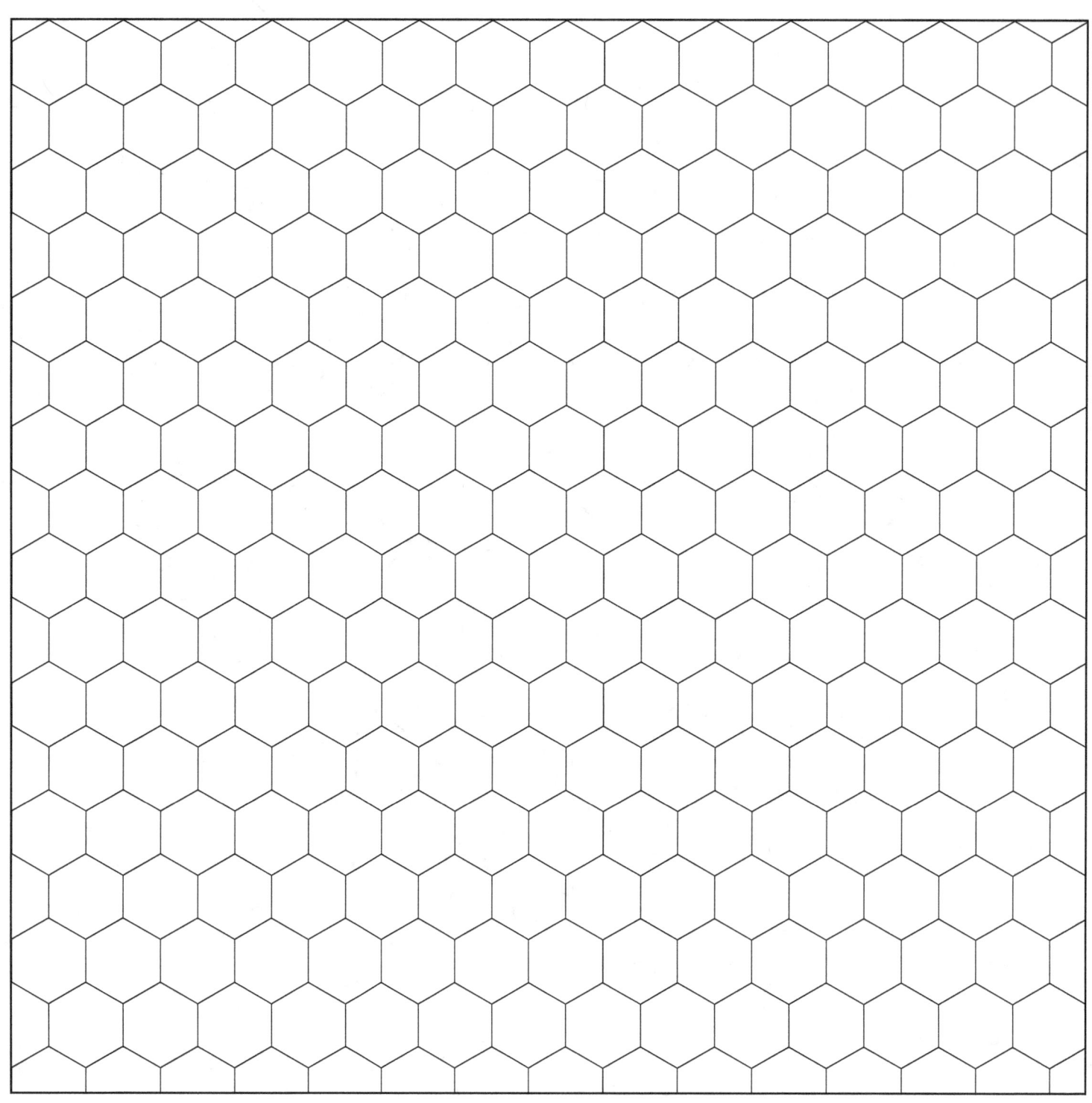

"Hope is the only bee that makes honey without flowers"
Robert Green Ingersoll

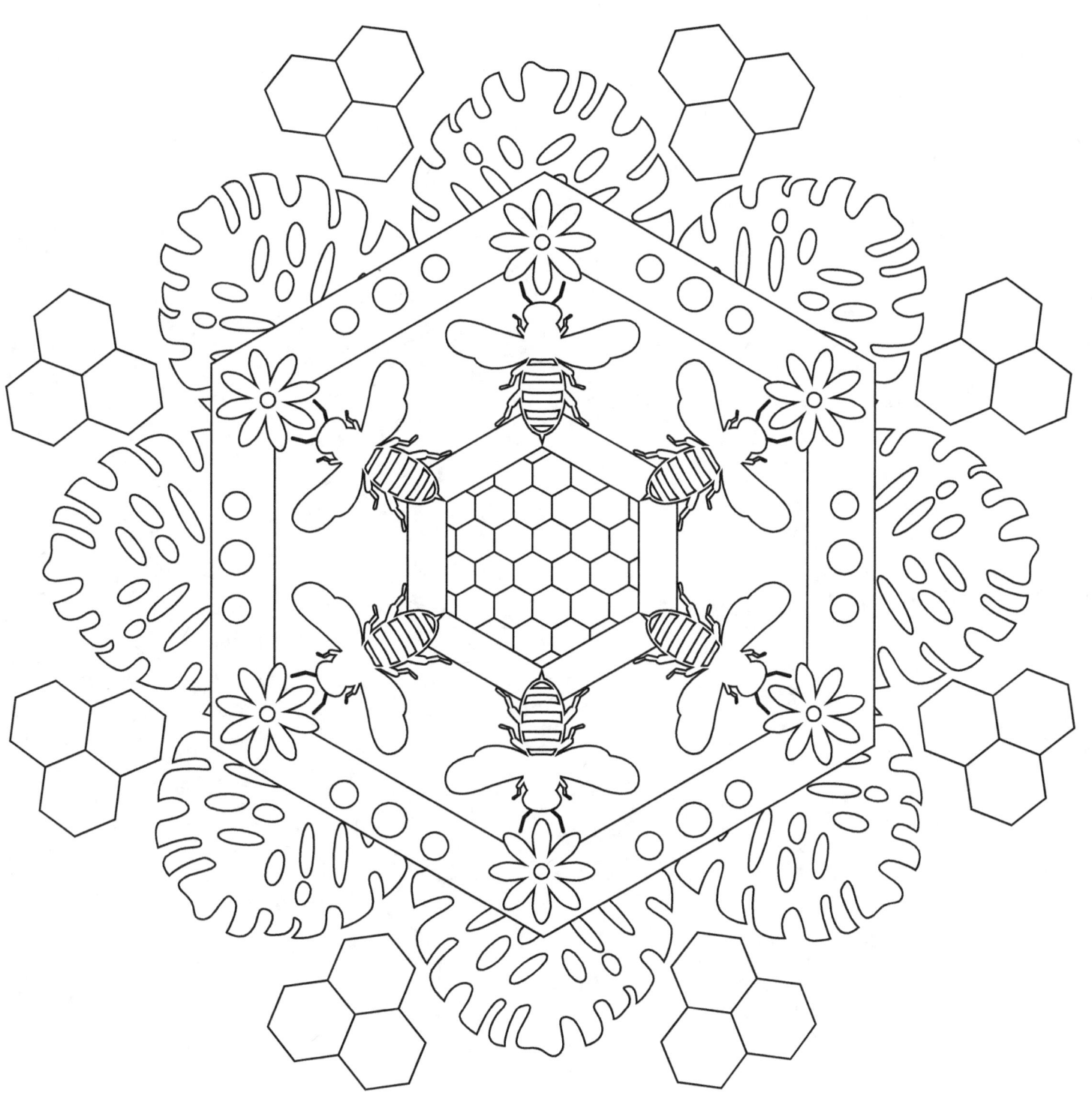

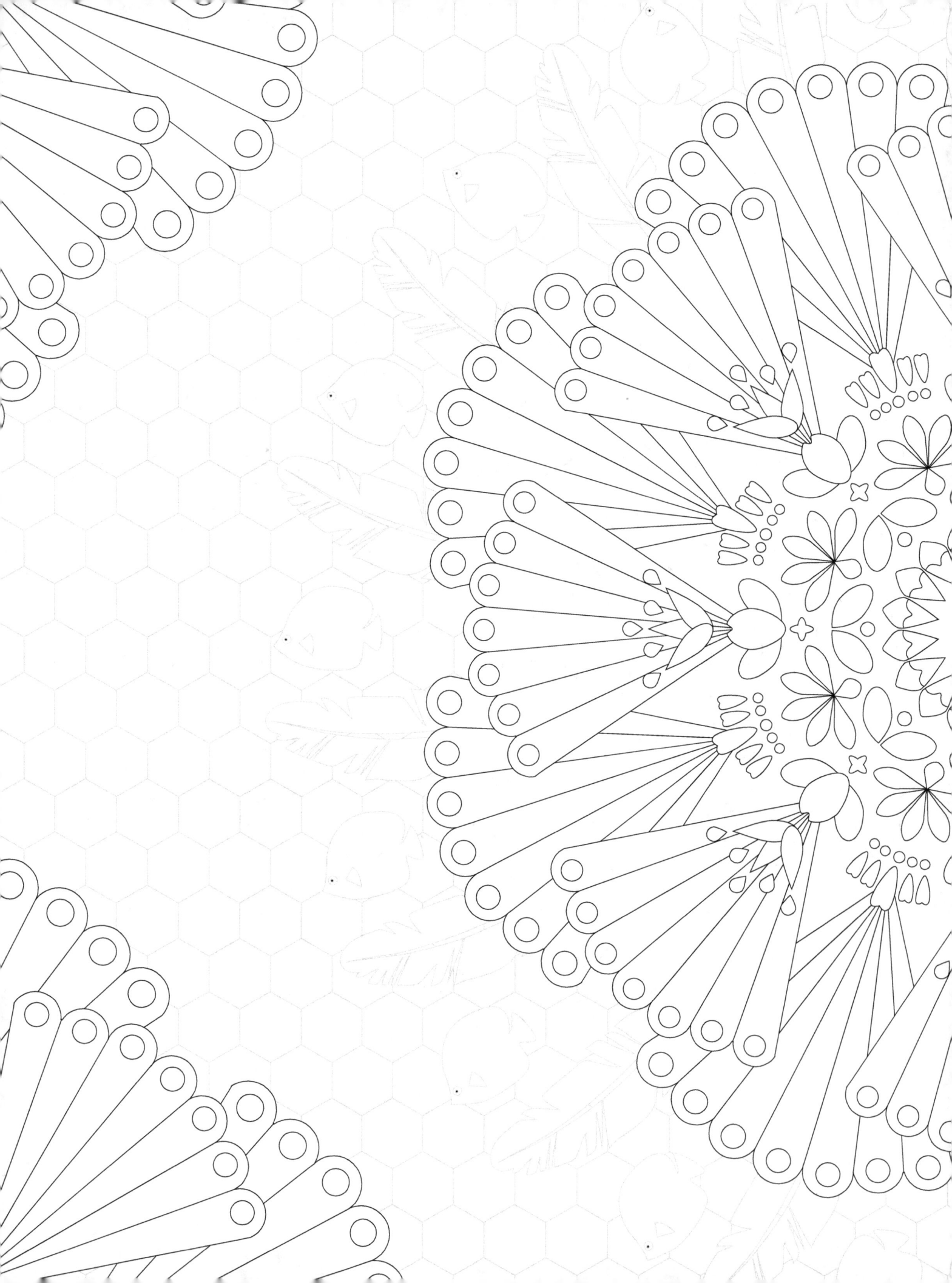